CRAZY LOVELY LIFE

CRAZY LOVELY LIFE

POETRY OF LOVE & PASSION

KAY WOODS

Photography & Illustrations
With use under license
Copyright © Shutterstock.com
Cover Photo: oneinchpunch/shutterstock.com

Author Photo, Back Cover
Cassidy Nunn/Nunn Other Photography
nunnotherphotography.com

Copyright © 2020 Kay Woods
All rights reserved.
ISBN: 978-1-7770987-0-4 (Print)
ISBN: 978-1-7770987-1-1 (EBook)

THIS COLLECTION IS DEDICATED TO:

*The Love of My Life
And My Closest Friend,
For Your Constant Support and Encouragement
To Be Nothing But Myself*

FOREWORD

I've always been blessed – *or should I say cursed?* – with the ability to feel much more deeply than others. This has made for an interesting journey so far, to say the least.

In growing up and finding myself, a large part of my identity became navigating the maze of mental wellness. Forever trying to find balance among the extremes of my life... *and it's been a wild ride.*

But I am a strong believer that our struggles teach us how to rise above.

And ever since, I've been on an eternal quest to find True Love. *Searching for that connection which would bring peace to my restless soul.*

And here we are. Which is why it feels right to release this collection at this time.

Newlywed and loving life, I decided to finally do something for me.

Thank you for choosing this book.

I truly hope that you will strike your own connection, for if you let them, these words will bleed passion and make their way into your heart.

Happy Reading,

TABLE OF CONTENTS

A Philosopher Once Said... 1

Lift Me Up... 3

Fragmented Thoughts | My Happy Place... 5

It Was Love... 7

Perfectly Whole... 8

Finally Free... 10

Captivated... 12

Hold Me Tight... 14

Be My Soldier... 16

To The One I Love... 19

Fairytale Ending... 21

By Your Side... 22

Hot Fudge Sundae... 24

Open Road... 26

Two Hearts... 29

The Best of Both Worlds... 31

Fragmented Thoughts | I'm Slipping... 32

The Land of Normal... 35

Labels... 36
Make Believe Happy... 38
A New Kind of Broken... 39
Both to Blame... 41
Dreaming of You... 43
Fragmented Thoughts | Trust, They Say... 44
Silver Linings... 46
It's You That I Crave... 49
Dreams... 50

Fragmented Thoughts | Wild Energy... 53
Believe In Me... 55
Screaming Colour... 56
Love Story... 57
My Anchor... 58
Like A Flower... 60
Break Free and Fly Away... 62
Dancer... 65
Fall... 67

Fragmented Thoughts | Think in Pictures... 69
Stolen Silence... 71
Bookstore Love... 72
Pitter Patter... 75
Never Say Goodbye... 76
Christmas... 79
Storybook Magic... 80
Live Free... 82
Ambition... 85
Stories Just Find Me... 87

About The Author... 89

A PHILOSOPHER ONCE SAID...

"You will never be happy if you continue to search for what happiness consists of. You will never live if you are looking for the meaning of life".

- Albert Camus

Vadym Sh/Shutterstock.com

LIFT ME UP

It was the way my body
Ached for you
And couldn't find the words
The way you lifted me up
And took away the hurt...

LilacHome/Shutterstock.com

FRAGMENTED THOUGHTS

It was the kind of love you only dreamed about. The total and utter belonging that can only come from a bond formed by tragedy. The lasting imprint of a person whose soul so closely aligns with your own; the overwhelming need to fight your demons together, and to
never again go it alone.

For this love – *this person* – is everything that you've ever secretly wished for, while being everything that you truly need. It's the laugh-out-loud moments and quiet embrace. That deep undivided connection…

My Happy Place

Emotions Studio/Shutterstock.com

IT WAS LOVE

It was in his touch
And the way he kissed me
It was the smell of him
And the way he missed me
... It was Love

PERFECTLY WHOLE

I fall deeply
And break easily
But always love strong
I thought this heart would never heal
But then you came along

It was in the quiet moments
The way you squeezed my hand
When you looked into my eyes
And always seemed to understand

It's how I tremble at your touch
The whispered words and stolen glances
That we loved so much

And suddenly
You had made me
Perfectly Whole
Like nothing inside was ever broken

That summer it was my heart you stole

FINALLY FREE

Wind in my hair
We were both just there
Standing on that beach

Finally Free

Together was still a mystery
But I found you
And you found me

Mimadeo/Shutterstock.com

CAPTIVATED

I long to learn
What has been
Painfully & Beautifully Written
On the pages of your soul

I long to know
The story of you

>   *What has been*
>   *What is*
>   *What was*

For with you
I am
Infatuated & Absolutely Captivated

Nadiia/Shutterstock.com

HOLD ME TIGHT

Hold me tight
Look into my eyes
Kiss these lips
Challenge my mind

Protect my heart
And feed my soul
Hold my hand
And support my goals

Make me laugh
Take me out to dance
Light this life on fire
Fill my world with romance

We'll share our secrets
And bare it all
I'll raise you up
You won't let me fall

You're my inspiration
My brilliant shining knight
The Prince that stole my heart
With just one kiss
On that first night

Masson/Shutterstock.com

BE MY SOLDIER

Be my shield
From prying eyes
The safe house
For my soul
Take my hand and wrap me up tight
You make my heart whole

Be that strong hand
When I'm slipping
Fighting all my fears
You brought me back to life
The part of me that was missing

Be my soldier
When I'm folding
Stand me up straight
You're my hero
And this is fate

GLRL/Shutterstock.com

Kokulina/Shutterstock.com

TO THE ONE I LOVE

To The One I Love
My soul found you
My missing piece
I will always be true

I hold you in my heart
You've become a part of me
Two lives became one
You are my destiny

My kiss on his lips
His lips on my skin
One hand in my hair
The other holding his

One moment in time
Let's stay here forever
It's true love's kiss
For Worse or For Better

Spixel/Shutterstock.com

FAIRYTALE ENDING

Look in my eyes
See the pain inside
See the pieces of a broken heart
And the nights I've cried

But that was until
You came into my life
Until our paths intertwined
Until you stood by my side
And your dreams became mine

Now look inside
And see my pride
See the hope
From a love that shines

So stay with me
Run away with me
This is my fairytale ending
And you've set me free

BY YOUR SIDE

Forever...
    Longing
        Wanting
            Hoping

To have just another minute
To be by your side
Feel your warmth
And hold on tight

Because it will never be long enough
To express my love

Rawpixxel.com/Shutterstock.com

HOT FUDGE SUNDAE

You're my hot fudge sundae
My walking in the rain
You're my sun
And my moon
The familiar hand that lights the way

You're my stars and my sky
You're my wings when I need to fly
You're my sunset on the water
And hot chocolate when it snows
My voice to speak up
When nobody else knows

You're my indulgence
And companion
My passion and my grace
You're my heart and soul
Kept warm with your embrace

You're my vision of beauty
Bringing contrast and delight
You always keep me going
With reassurance and courage
The excitement of never knowing

You're every new experience
Sharing the same dreams
Each and every day
Giving me reasons to believe

OPEN ROAD

It's an overwhelming need
A desire to be free
There's passion inside
A longing to know
What's on the other side

It's a drive to see the world
And the road is calling me
Amazing places to go and see
All the while
You right beside me

It's these times I love you most
When you understand my urge to go
That it's a passion for travel
Not an unhappiness with home

Kisses at the red light
Moonlit nights and backseat fights

Let's run away together
Foster a love so great
That it begs for adventure

It's time to enjoy one another
Because this is our forever

Ann Patchanan/Shutterstock.com

chainarong06/Shutterstock.com

TWO HEARTS

It's as if my arms
Fit perfectly around you
The space between
Melting beneath
As if it had never existed

Leaving Only

Two hearts
Beating hard
To fill the silence
Of a love like ours

Portb/Shutterstock.com

THE BEST OF BOTH WORLDS

It was then
All of a sudden
We were no longer two roads

But one

Now I trust you so completely
It almost scares me
Like winning the lottery
And you're there to share it with me

To be totally consumed
Yet feel so free
The companion and storybook ending
I'd always dreamed

So to you...
My Best Friend
And Partner in Crime

We have the best of both worlds
I'm Yours and You're Mine

FRAGMENTED THOUGHTS

With wonder and carefree spontaneity came moments of irresistible delight. Inevitably followed by the crushing deflate – the crash that accompanies such irresponsible ventures was waiting on the horizon. Patiently waiting to turn my world upside down. Like every time was the first. And yet the panicked reaction is the same; like I haven't been on this ride numerous times. Like I'm losing it.

Again – I'm slipping...

When your world is based on instability, we find ways to cope. When this life throws up disappointment, we keep trudging. Even when your next turn leads you down the wrong path, we're strong enough to know we've strayed, and long to find our way back.

But this life is as loopy as *Candyland*, and you never really know what's coming next.

So spin me, shake me, try to break me
Because I won't go down without a fight.

Lilawa.com/Shutterstock.com

THE LAND OF NORMAL

Fragile are we
When we rely on others opinions of beauty
Other opinions of what we are
Or what we should be

Could it be?
That 'Normal' is a world I created
Battling through stages
That others couldn't see

I used to think it wasn't fair
The struggle; This story
But it was a world of my own making
For I do not know a single person
Who grew up There

LABELS

It sticks forever
Being labeled young
The struggle is my story
But I've learned to rise above

Being burned
Makes it hard to trust
Because these labels –
They define us

So don't call me crazy, mad, or insane
Those are just words
But this isn't a game

Why can't I just be me...?
But you live with it so long
You're left asking
Is this my identity?

So please be patient
Be sure to be kind
And don't be so quick to judge
Because those labels...
They never really leave us

Albina Tiplyashina/Shutterstock.com

MAKE BELIEVE HAPPY

Maybe tonight's the night
That you make my heart ache
The very last time
You take my breath away

Maybe this is it
What I've been waiting for
Make believe happy
With one foot out the door

Just a hopeless romance
Living in the past
Reaching out to you
When I knew this love would never last

A NEW KIND OF BROKEN

My body can't handle it
Yet how I've tried
You used me all up
And this love was a lie

Time heals wounds
But I've been waiting years
This is a new kind of broken
And I can't stop the tears

Frankie's/Shutterstock.com

BOTH TO BLAME

Hit by a hurricane
My life turned again

Both to Blame

But it just wasn't right
And that won't change

So I followed my heart
To rise above
Find courage and strength
To once again
Fall in Love

AlexandCo Studio/Shutterstock.com

DREAMING OF YOU

My heart skips a beat
But can't find the words
Dreaming of you
But don't have the courage
To let you in
So you can see
Exactly
How much you mean to me

But little do I know
You feel it too
Both too nervous to tell the truth

You're the one that I desire
Send this friendship up in smoke
And light my world on fire

FRAGMENTED THOUGHTS

Trust, they say.
Have faith.
Things will work out.

As if it were as easy as that.

But yet we try...
Try to mold a life we thought was right.
As if it were ever our decision in the first place.
And in the end we fall.
Or crumple under the stress of it all.

But then I met you.

And everything was different.
Everything was new.
You were the life I was waiting for.

But here we are. In the same familiar place.
Where the problem wasn't life at all – *but me.*
I was the one who needed to change.
Blinded by it all. Running from impatience.
Always trying to force pieces that never fit.
Now I've got it right – and yet…
The world is forcing me to wait.
Have faith.

The difference; however,
in this case
*It's **You** that's worth waiting for.*

SILVER LININGS

In this life
I've had to find enough

Silver linings

To build a set of armour
For my shining knight
Dreaming of a fairytale ending
I got stuck with this life

Although things worth waiting for take time
Find me in this tower
Come and dry these tears of mine

It's you that can make me believe

Where others have drowned
You brought a boat
There's no brick wall around this heart
Just a moat

Tomorrow is a new day
And a chance at adventure awaits

For you I'd lower the bridge
And welcome you in

Just a girl in a skyscraper
Looking for her Prince

Nikita Bulanov/Shutterstock.com

IT'S YOU THAT I CRAVE

When I'm reaching to the clouds
Reaching out of bounds
You bring me back
In this manic life
It's hard to stay on track

You challenge my fears
And keep my feet on the ground
You keep me focused
And calm me down

You soothe my soul
Every single day
You've changed my life
And now it's you that I crave

DREAMS

Now I lay me down to sleep
I pray tonight
The dreams don't find me

Sleeping with you
Is the only way
They may come
But you always wake

There's no need to be afraid
It's by your side
That I feel safe

Rawpixel.com/Shutterstock.com

Palo_ok/Shutterstock.com

FRAGMENTED THOUGHTS

She was the kind of wild energy that longed for real belonging.

*The kind of girl that **spoke up** and **stuck out**, living on the edge of reality and madness.*

Forever grasping at making memories that would ultimately be lost among throes of heartbreak.

A life that struggle defines...

Lilawa.com/Shutterstock.com

BELIEVE IN ME

I may be a thousand good intentions
Sometimes with no plan
But the desire to run in any direction
Just to know that I can

Constantly fighting to quiet my mind
Bound by my own limitations
Slowly finding my feet
But built on a rocky foundation

I want to shed this darkness
But battle with it every day
Please see the happiness behind my tears
And help to show me the way

It is with you I feel
That – *finally* – I can breathe
No longer hiding
Or afraid to be me

Yet I may sometimes show
The worst parts of myself
I truly wish you'd see
That this has changed everything

Because you Believe In Me

SCREAMING COLOR

In Screaming Color
You've seen my soul
Erased my fears
And supported my goals

You've gotten so close
To see the *real me*
Broken down these walls
And learnt my identity

LOVE STORY

I am formed by fragments of quotes
Where song lyrics fill in the gaps
Living in the chapters of a book
Lost on a winding path

There's nothing that hasn't already been said
No words that haven't already been read
But in this life of black and white text
It's our love story that comes next

4Max/Shutterstock.com

MY ANCHOR

You're the anchor
That keeps me on the ground
You're my shining light
When I'm shadowed by dark clouds

You're my strength
When I'm running low on hope
You're the source of courage
That's keeping me afloat

You soothe a heart that's hard to please
For you I would cross a thousand seas

I want you to know
I'll be by your side
Through good times and bad
High and low tide

This journey hasn't been easy
But we'll weather the storm together
Keep me warm
And we'll ride these waves forever

Like a boat to my lighthouse
A moth to a flame
You will have my heart
Until my dying day

Jarkko Mattheiszen/Shutterstock.com

LIKE A FLOWER

Like a flower needs the sun
You're the one
In this stormy world
You make my heart jump

When night falls
Morning will come
It can feel like forever
But it always does

It's these times
I need you most
And you're always by my side
Whenever I am plagued by doubt
You pull me back into the light

Like a flower
Retreating into darkness
When the day is done
The only thing that keeps me going
Is promise of the sun

Like a flower loves the rain
You make me feel
Like I need you
You make me real

You've given me a life
That's as good as it can be
By your side forever
You set my heart free

BREAK FREE & FLY AWAY

Until I was grown
Home was home
The complete and steady center of my world
Little did I know
That when I was ready
That world turned

It was only a feeling
A longing and a need
To find my own path
To meander and wander
Where others had
To travel and experience
Faraway lands

When there's something stronger
Than your reason to stay
Don't be afraid to

Break Free & Fly Away

Always follow your heart
Because goodbye never means
You won't be back someday

Min C. Chiu/Shutterstock.com

Valenty/Shutterstock.com

DANCER

When she Dances
She loses herself
And forgets the world

Her body breathes the music
And her heart knows all the lines

That passion inside is set free

This is

Exactly

Where she is meant to be

Dmitryp-k/Shutterstock.com

FALL

There's something about fall
That puts a spring in my step
The summer just ending
With no regrets...

Brisk morning air
Take a deep breath

The changing of the season
Pushes for a change in me
Craving a new challenge
And a new beginning

Follow your dreams
Crunch some leaves
Take some time
To make yourself happy

When one door closes
We must move on

Dream Big; Live Fast; Change Often

Kamira/Shutterstock.com

FRAGMENTED THOUGHTS

I seem to think in pictures...

With one flash comes so much story.
One that would take forever to turn into words.
And then another. And another.

Until I'm so far down the rabbit hole that there's no rope long enough to pull me out.

*It's like seeing colour
in a black and white world.*

Where others are learning to read – I have movies.
So much thought. So much detail. So much worry.
To constantly experience – *to feel* – that which cannot be explained. Just known.
I don't know how else to be.
How to think simply.
Sometimes I'm grateful – and often tired...
But this is me.

And sometimes I just wish I could turn off the TV.

Pablo Rogat/Shutterstock.com

STOLEN SILENCE

In those moments near early dawn
Tea in hand
Morning yawn
She finds herself
Taken with the silence

Profound and echoing
While the entire house sleeps
Consuming thoughts
And peaceful quiet
While the rest dream

The anomaly to a busy life
This *Stolen Silence*
Which always seems to quiet
The storm inside her mind

BOOKSTORE LOVE

The door creaks open
The bell chimes above
The dusty smell reaches me
This is bookstore love

SvedOliver/Shutterstock.com

The tall shelves wind deep inside
Through, around, in and behind
Filled with endless stories
To challenge my mind

A million worlds
In one small shop
Black and white brilliance
Thoughtful plots

My favourite memories
Are of places like this
Rummaging through shelves
Finding a place to sit

Enjoy the process
And take home a treasure
That book may be passed on
But these memories last forever

Evgeni Kolesnik/Shutterstock.com

PITTER PATTER

It's the pitter patter
Of little feet
The love and laughter
That make children so sweet

Big hearts
And unspoiled dreams
Dress up parties
And endless energy

It's the miracle of life
Held in my arms
I promise forever
To protect you from harm

NEVER SAY GOODBYE

We never spent much time together
Neither did I try
I want to say I'm sorry
But not to say goodbye

I never got to know you
Although I told myself I would
It just didn't feel right
But I knew it could

I was a little scared of you
I don't really know why
I wanted to show you I love you
But I didn't really try

Before I knew it my time was up
Dead like a flower under the dry hot sun

If I knew when I saw you it would be my last
It would have been different
It wouldn't have been so fast

I'm sorry I didn't spend more time with you
I'm sorry I didn't try
For if I knew it was my last
I would have put my hesitation aside

I love you very much
And wanted you to know
Please forgive me for this
That only now I show

I know you're up there smiling
I know you're up there waiting
Someday we will meet again
So I promise not to say goodbye until then.

Str33t cat/Shutterstock.com

*For my late grandmother, may she rest in peace.
This was one of the very first poems I ever wrote.
Even at twelve years old I knew the power of words...
Writing has always been my passion.*

CHRISTMAS

Christmas Lights
Shining Bright
From the first crackling fire
Until you take that last bite

Happiness is found
Singing out loud
With friends and family
Gathered around

Smiles and stuffed stockings
Childish delight
Warmed hearts
And hot chocolate
On this frosty night

Cookies, carols, and
Love in the air
This Season
Is the reason
We hold Christmas so dear

STORYBOOK MAGIC

It's here you'll find me
With a good book and warm tea
Bundled up beneath the sheets

Tucked in tight
But I'll be up all night
For the love of a good story
Don't turn out the light

Clever words can seduce the soul
Take you to places you've never known
Teach lessons that can't just be told

Bringing magic and mystery
With curious delight
Tall tales that twist, engage, and entice

Because there's just some things
That screens can't do
They can't hold coffee stains,
Spilt tears, or these memories of you

They can't hold pressed flowers
Amidst their pages
No handwritten notes
To be treasured by future generations

It's here you'll find me
And I'll stay true...

*Of course, my dear
Only real books will do.*

Vadym Sh/Shutterstock.com

LIVE FREE

In a lesson not soon forgotten
It was my grandmother
Who once taught me
What it means to be *truly free*

Free from your ideals
Of what should be
Of what you need it to be
That life just happens –
Everything for a reason

She was the one that showed me

When the cage is finally broken
This is all you need

Patience, my dear. Just patience.

What's meant to be
Will be...

The Italians phrase it beautifully
'Vivere Liberamente'
Live Free

Frankie's/Shutterstock.com

NiE PROJECT/Shutterstock.com

AND THAT'S WHAT I CALL AMBITION...

If we're both looking down the path of life
We both have an end
We both see that end

Mine is at the end of a long road

I'm standing on one side
Staring down the path
Runners on; Ready to go

You're on the other side
You have an end
You can see that end

But in the middle is a large gap

But You...

Instead of *finding your feet*
And making your own way

You're just falling...

Desperately trying to put your shoes on

Christos Georghiou/Shutterstock.com

STORIES JUST FIND ME

Writing, It Motivates Me
Words, They Flow Through Me
Memories, They Bind Me
Stories Just Find Me

ABOUT THE AUTHOR

She grew up a dancer; a writer; a fighter.

Transfixed with words from a young age, she writes as an outlet for the passion, bubbling just beneath the surface.

She thinks obsessively, writes fervently, and the words just spill over – somehow forming graceful notions from the hurricane inside her mind.

Living the Island Life with her Husband and Pup on the beautiful West Coast, she's a friend, a traveler, and a romantic at heart.

She spends her days in the corporate world – organized, professional, precise...

But her heart lives in the creative world – writing, planning, dancing...

Finally taking some time to follow her passions, she shares her thoughts on the experience of love and life.

Find the complete works at:

KayWoodsPublishing.com

Manufactured by Amazon.ca
Bolton, ON